LISTS TO LIVE BY

for

SIMPLE LIVING

COMPILED BY ALICE GRAY,
STEVE STEPHENS, JOHN VAN DIEST

Multnomah® Publishers *Sisters, Oregon*

D0292687

LISTS TO LIVE BY FOR SIMPLE LIVING
published by Multnomah Publishers, Inc.
© 2002 by Alice Gray, Steve Stephens, John Van Diest
International Standard Book Number: 1-59052-058-0

Cover image by David Uttley/UDG DesignWorks
Cover image by Photodisc

Scripture quotations are from:
The Holy Bible, New International Version © 1973, 1984 by International
Bible Society, used by permission of Zondervan Publishing House

Other Scripture quotations:

The Holy Bible, King James Version (KJV)

The New Testament in Modern English, Revised Edition (PHILLIPS)
© 1958, 1960, 1972 by J. B. Phillips

The New English Bible (NEB) © 1970 by
Oxford University Press and Cambridge University Press

Holy Bible, New Living Translation (NLT) © 1996.
Used by permission of Tyndale House Publishers, Inc.

Multnomah is a trademark of Multnomah Publishers, Inc.,
and is registered in the U.S. Patent and Trademark Office.
The colophon is a trademark of Multnomah Publishers, Inc.

Printed in the United States of America

For information:
MULTNOMAH PUBLISHERS, INC., POST OFFICE BOX 1720
SISTERS, OREGON 97759

Lists to live by for simple living / compiled by Alice Gray, Steve Stephens, John Van Diest.
  p. cm.
  ISBN 1-59052-058-0
    1. Simplicity--Miscellanea. 2. Conduct of life--Miscellanea. I. Gray, Alice, 1939-
II. Stephens, Steve. III. Van Diest, John.

BJ1496 .L575 2002
646.7--dc21

2002005975

02 03 04 05 06 07 08—10 9 8 7 6 5 4 3 2 1 0

LISTS TO LIVE BY

—— *for* ——

SIMPLE LIVING

Books in the Lists to Live By series:

Lists to Live By: The First Collection

Lists to Live By: The Second Collection

Lists to Live By: The Third Collection

Lists to Live By: The Fourth Collection (December 2002)

Lists to Live By for Every Married Couple

Lists to Live By for Every Caring Family

Lists to Live By for Smart Living

Lists to Live By for Simple Living

Contents

Introduction

Stillness
    Harmony
        Gentleness
           Peace

Just the sound of these words brings comfort. But in our fast-paced, complex world, how do we find the simple path? Or we might even ask if such a path truly exists. The wonderful answer is yes.

The gateway to the path of living simply is found in the collection you currently hold. The beauty of these thoughtfully chosen lists is that they use simplicity to bring you simplicity.

So sit back, put your feet up and enjoy a gentle pace that will…

Relax your body.

Ease your mind.

Calm your heart.

Enrich your spirit.

—ALICE GRAY, DR. STEVE STEPHENS, AND JOHN VAN DIEST

Things to Feel Nostalgic About

A barefoot walk along a sandy beach.

A quiet visit to the place where you were raised.

Listening to a rippling brook running
over the rocks through a forest of autumn leaves.

Singing the song of your alma mater.

Looking over childhood photos in the family album.

Watching your now-grown child leave home.

Standing silently beside the grave
of a close personal friend or relative.

The smell and sounds of a warm fire.

An old letter, bruised with age, signed by one who loved you.

Climbing to the top of a wind-swept hill.

Getting alone—all alone—and reading aloud.

Christmas Eve, late at night.

Certain poems…certain melodies.

Weddings…graduations…diplomas.

Snow…sleds…toboggans.

Saying good-bye.

CHARLES R. SWINDOLL
From *Growing Strong in the Seasons of Life*

The Optimist Creed

Commit yourself:

- To be so strong that nothing can disturb your peace of mind.

- To talk health, happiness, and prosperity to every person you meet.

- To make all your friends feel that there is something special in them.

- To look at the sunny side of everything and make your optimism come true.

- To think only of the best, to work only for the best, and to expect only the best.

- To be just as enthusiastic about the success of others as you are about your own.

- To forget the mistakes of the past and press on to the greater achievements of the future.

- To wear a cheerful countenance at all times and give every living creature you meet a smile.

- To give so much time to the improvement of yourself that you have no time to criticize others.

- To be too large for worry, too noble for anger, too strong for fear, and too happy to permit the presence of trouble.

OPTIMIST INTERNATIONAL®

Avoid Getting and Doing Too Much

- Is this really important to me?

- Do I truly enjoy this?

- Do I really need this?

- Does this cause stress and drain my energy?

- Does this cause me to hurry too much?

- What are healthier alternatives?

- How did I manage without this?

ROBERT AND DEBRA BRUCE AND ELLEN OLDACRE
From *Standing Up against the Odds*

One Is Poor If He...

Cannot enjoy what he has.

Is not content.

Is short on good works.

Has no self-respect.

Has no real friends.

Has lost the zest for living.

Has little joy.

Has lost his health.

Has no eternal hope.

LEROY BROWNLOW
Condensed from *A Psalm in My Heart*

The Greatest Things

The best day, today;

The greatest puzzle, life;

The greatest thought, God;

The greatest mystery, death;

The best work, work you like;

The most ridiculous asset, pride;

The greatest need, common sense;

The most expensive indulgence, hate;

The most disagreeable person, the complainer;

The best teacher, the one who makes you want to learn;

The greatest deceiver, the one who deceives himself;

The worst bankruptcy, the soul who has lost enthusiasm;

The cheapest, easiest, and most stupid thing to do, finding fault;

The greatest comfort, the knowledge that you have done
your work well;

The most agreeable companion, the one who would not
have you any different than you are;

The meanest feeling, being envious of another's success;

The greatest thing in the world, love—for family, home, friends,
neighbors.

AUTHOR UNKNOWN

Tranquility

* You can have peace in your heart with little if you are in the will of God, but you can be miserable with much if you are out of His will.

* You can have joy in obscurity if you are in the will of God, but you can be wretched with wealth and fame out of His will.

* You can be happy in the midst of sufferings if you are in God's will, but you can have agony in good health out of His will.

* You can be contented in poverty if you are in the will of God, but you can be wretched in riches out of His will.

* You can be calm and at peace in the midst of persecution as long as you are in the will of God, but you can be miserable and defeated in the midst of acclaim if you are out of His will.

BILLY GRAHAM
From *Unto the Hills*

Gift of Simplicity

THE GIFT OF SILENCE:

*Quieting my voice so
I can be refreshed by the stillness for
which my spirit desperately longs.*

Ten Rules to Live By

1. Count your blessings.

2. Today, and every day, deliver more than you are getting paid to do.

3. Whenever you make a mistake or get knocked down by life, don't look back at it too long.

4. Always reward your long hours of labor and toil in the very best way, surrounded by your family.

5. Build this day on a foundation of pleasant thoughts.

6. Live this day as if it will be your last.

7. Laugh at yourself and at life.

8. Never neglect the little things.

9. Welcome every morning with a smile.

10. Search for the seed of good in every adversity.

OG MANDINO
From *A Better Way to Live*

Simple Abundance

1. Health enough to make work a pleasure

2. Wealth enough to support your needs

3. Strength enough to battle difficulties and overcome them

4. Grace enough to confess your sins and forsake them

5. Patience enough to toil until some good is accomplished

6. Clarity enough to see some good in your neighbor

7. Love enough to move you to be useful and helpful to others

8. Faith enough to make real the things of God

9. Hope enough to remove all anxious fears confronting the future

GOETHE
Poet, playwright, and novelist

18 Ways to Feel Better

1. Call a friend.

2. Drive to the supermarket and
buy fresh flowers for your kitchen table.

3. Give someone a compliment.

4. Eat five bites of something rich and fattening and delicious.

5. Put on your favorite CD and dance.

6. Sit on the porch and drink tea from your most elegant china.

7. Do one thing you've been putting off for months.

8. Plant something.

9. Take a mini-vacation.

10. Rekindle your dreams.

11. Simplify your life.

12. Protect your privacy.

13. Forgive someone who hurt you.

14. Guard your thoughts.

15. Take care of your body.

16. Tend to your soul.

17. Write in your journal.

18. Pray for your friends and family.

KAREN SCALF LINAMEN

Condensed from

Sometimes I Wake Up Grumpy…and Sometimes I Let Him Sleep

The ability to simplify
means to eliminate the unnecessary
so that the necessary may speak.
—HANS HOFFMAN

There is no power on earth that can neutralize
the influence of a high, simple, and useful life.
—BOOKER T. WASHINGTON

I love tranquil solitude
And such society
As is quiet, wise, and good.
—PERCY B. SHELLEY

What Simplicity Does

Eases our stress

Clears away our clutter

Increases our appreciation

Clarifies our priorities

Purifies our hearts

Uplifts our spirits

Settles our emotions

Encourages our friends

Deepens our peace

Builds our character

DR. STEVE STEPHENS
Psychologist and seminar speaker

What Prayer Does

Washes away faults

Repels temptations

Extinguishes persecutions

Consoles the fainthearted

Cheers the low-spirited

Escorts travelers

Nourishes the poor

Governs the rich

Raises up the fallen

Arrests the falling

Confirms the standing

TERTULLIAN
First-century lawyer and teacher

Gift of Simplicity

THE GIFT OF CONTENTMENT:

*Being thankful for
what I have instead of striving for
what I don't have.*

Symphony of Contentment

To live content with small means;

To seek elegance rather than luxury, and refinement rather than fashion;

To be worthy, not respectable, and wealthy, not rich;

To study hard, think quietly, talk gently, act frankly;

To listen to stars and birds, to babes and sages, with open heart;

To bear all cheerfully, do all bravely, await occasions, hurry never.

In a word, to let the spiritual, unbidden and unconscious, grow up through the common.

This is to be my symphony.

WILLIAM HENRY CHANNING
Chaplain during the Civil War

12 Treasures for Happiness

Always be honest.

Count your blessings.

Bear each other's burdens.

Forgive and forget.

Be kind and tenderhearted.

Comfort one another.

Keep your promises.

Be supportive of one another.

Be true to each other.

Look after each other.

Treat all others as you treat your friends.

But most important, love one another deeply from the heart.

SELECTED FROM *The Holy Bible*

Wise Sayings My Mother Taught Me

A thing of beauty is a joy forever.

It's always darkest just before the dawn.

Big oaks from little acorns grow.

God never gives more than you can bear.

This, too, shall pass.

Can't never did anything.

Nothing ventured, nothing gained.

A man is known by the friends he keeps.

Still waters run deep.

All the flowers of tomorrow are in the seeds of today.

NOLA BERTELSON
Wife, mother, and grandmother

Perfect Days

JUST FOR TODAY

I will try to strengthen my mind by reading something that requires effort, thought, and concentration.

JUST FOR TODAY

I will do somebody a good turn and not get found out.

JUST FOR TODAY

I will do a task that needs to be done but which I have been putting off. I will do it as an exercise in willpower.

JUST FOR TODAY

I will dress as becomingly as possible, talk low, act courteously, be liberal with praise, and neither criticize one bit nor find fault with anything.

JUST FOR TODAY

I will have a quiet half hour all by myself and relax. In this half hour I will think of God so as to get more perspective in my life.

JUST FOR TODAY

I will be unafraid. Especially, I will not be afraid to be happy, to enjoy what is beautiful, to love, and to believe that those I love, love me.

AUTHOR UNKNOWN

The World Needs People...

Who cannot be bought;

Whose word is their bond;

Who put character above wealth;

Who possess opinions and a will;

Who are larger than their vocations;

Who do not hesitate to take chances;

Who will not lose their individuality in a crowd;

Who will be as honest in small things as in great things;

Who will make no compromise with wrong;

Whose ambitions are not confined to their own selfish desires;

Who will not say they do it "because everybody else does it";

Who are true to their friends through good report and evil report, in adversity as well as prosperity;

Who do not believe that shrewdness, cunning, and hardheadedness are the best qualities for winning success;

Who are not ashamed or afraid to stand for the truth when it is unpopular;

Who can say "no" with emphasis, although all the rest of the world says "yes."

TED W. ENGSTROM
From *Motivation to Last a Lifetime*

The Best of Virtue

Love means to love that which is unlovable,

or it is no virtue at all.

Forgiving means to pardon the unpardonable,

or it is no virtue at all.

Faith means believing the unbelievable,

or it is no virtue at all.

Hope means hoping when things are hopeless,

or it is no virtue at all.

ADAPTED FROM G. K. CHESTERTON

novelist, poet, and essayist

Gift of Simplicity

THE GIFT OF TODAY:

Rejoicing in today instead of borrowing trouble from tomorrow or rehearsing the regrets of yesterday.

Let Us Learn by Paradox...

That the way down is the way up,

That to be low is to be high,

That the broken heart is the healed heart,

That the contrite spirit is the rejoicing spirit,

That the repenting soul is the victorious soul,

That to have nothing is to possess all.

ARTHUR BENNETT
From *The Valley of Vision*

Choices

→ If you want to be rich...GIVE

→ If you want to be poor...GRASP

→ If you want abundance...SCATTER

→ If you want to be needy...HOARD

JOHN LAWRENCE
From *The Seven Laws of the Harvest*

Wisdom for Simple Living

We should all consider:
"A little more kindness and a little less greed;
a little more giving and a little less need."
—C. Austin Miles

I have simply tried to do what
seemed best each day, as each day came.
—Abraham Lincoln

Life would be tragically limited
if one could not live by faith.
—Richard C. Halverson

What Money Can and Cannot Buy

A bed but not sleep.

Books but not brains.

Food but not appetite.

Finery but not beauty.

A house but not a home.

Medicine but not health.

Luxuries but not culture.

Amusements but not happiness.

Companions but not friends.

Flattery but not respect.

AUTHOR UNKNOWN

Ten Wondrous Delights

1. The beauty of nature

2. The miracle of a newborn

3. The joy of discovery

4. The awesomeness of God

5. The thrill of accomplishment

6. The passion of love

7. The power of music

8. The deliciousness of food

9. The appreciation of life

10. The surprise of a gift

DR. STEVE STEPHENS
Psychologist and seminar speaker

Gift of Simplicity

THE GIFT OF JOY:

*Celebrating all
that is good and right and
beautiful in the world.*

I Am Thankful For...

...the mess to clean after a party because it means I have been surrounded by friends.

...the taxes I pay because it means I'm employed.

...the clothes that fit a little too snug because it means I have enough to eat.

...my shadow who watches me work because it means I am out in the sunshine.

...a lawn that needs mowing, windows that need cleaning, and gutters that need fixing because it means I have a home.

...the spot I find at the far end of the parking lot because it means I am capable of walking.

…all the complaining I hear about our government because it means we have freedom of speech.

…my huge heating bill because it means I am warm.

…the lady behind me in church who sings off-key because it means I can hear.

…the alarm that goes off in the early morning hours because it means I'm alive.

…the piles of laundry and ironing because it means my loved ones are nearby.

…weariness and aching muscles at the end of the day because it means I have been productive.

NANCIE J. CARMODY
From *Family Circle* magazine

Do Less

- Do less thinking,

  and pay more attention to your heart.

- Do less acquiring,

  and pay more attention to what you already have.

- Do less complaining,

  and pay more attention to giving.

- Do less controlling,

  and pay more attention to letting go.

- Do less criticizing,

  and pay more attention to complimenting.

- Do less arguing,

  and pay more attention to forgiveness.

- Do less running around,

  and pay more attention to stillness.

- Do less talking,

  and pay more attention to silence.

LEE L. JAMPOLSKY
Reprinted from *Smile for No Good Reason*

Seize the Day

- When you have the choice between taking an escalator or the stairs, take the stairs.

- Place fresh flowers in the places where you live and work.

- Visit the Holy Land once in your life.

- Smile at babies.

- When you develop your film, get double prints. Give the duplicates away.

- Remember, there is time for love and a place for love. Anytime, anyplace.

- Always go the extra mile…whether for a friend or for mint-chocolate ice cream.

- Whenever you look back on your life, be positive.

- If you seek wisdom over opportunity, opportunity will usually follow.

- Change is a process, not an event.

- Plan to be spontaneous.

- Whenever you look ahead, be optimistic.

- Enjoy each day as if it were your last.

BRUCE BICKEL AND STAN JANTZ
From *God Is in the Small Stuff...and It All Matters*

Gift of Simplicity

THE GIFT OF OTHERS:

Being truly happy
about the good fortune of others
and rejoicing with them.

Six Types of Love

1. Hold-me-close love

2. Crazy-about-me love

3. Give-me-limits love

4. Show-me-and-tell-me love

5. Play-with-me love

6. Help-me-hope love

ELISA MORGAN AND CAROL KUYKENDALL
From *What Every Child Needs*

Without Love...

All I say is ineffective

All I know is incomplete

All I believe is insufficient

All I give is insignificant

All I accomplish is inadequate

DR. MARK BELOKONNY
Pastor and teacher
Adapted from 1 Corinthians 13:1–3

Wisdom for Simple Living

*Simplicity is the economy of words
mixed with quality of thought
held together by subtlety of expression.*

—CHARLES SWINDOLL

*There are only two ways to live your life:
One is as though nothing is a miracle.
The other is as though everything is a miracle.*

—ALBERT EINSTEIN

*The best and most beautiful things
in life cannot be seen or even touched…
they must be felt with the heart.*

—HELEN KELLER

Leave It to God

Can't seem to get where you want to go fast enough?

Leave it to God.

Worried about the kids?

Leave it to God.

Living in a place you'd rather not be?

Leave it to God.

Looks like you won't graduate with honors?

Leave it to God.

No matter how hard you try, your life's partner is simply not responding?

Leave it to God.

Found a lump, and you see the doctor tomorrow?

Leave it to God.

CHARLES R. SWINDOLL
From *The Finishing Touch*

Winning Over Worry

1. Don't give up. Hope in God.

2. Walk by faith, not by sight.

3. Take time out for a good laugh.

4. Use the Bible as a window to see your world.

5. Never trouble trouble until trouble troubles you.

6. Make choices based on God's Word.

7. Give thanks to the Lord, for He is good.

8. Ask for God's strength to get you through.

9. Stop and enjoy the moment.

10. Pray as if everything depended upon God—it does.

LINDA SHEPHERD
From *Love's Little Recipes for Life*

Choose to...

Choose to love...rather than hate.

Choose to smile...rather than frown.

Choose to build...rather than destroy.

Choose to persevere...rather than quit.

Choose to praise...rather than gossip.

Choose to heal...rather than wound.

Choose to give...rather than grasp.

Choose to act...rather than delay.

Choose to forgive...rather than curse.

Choose to pray...rather than despair.

AUTHOR UNKNOWN

LISTS TO LIVE BY

The Simplest Pleasures

* Get up early enough to enjoy the wonder of a sunrise in leisure.

* Find a bench at the nearest park. Enjoy an entire thermos of coffee without interruption.

* Notice the intricate beauty of spiderwebs, pinecones, or icicles.

* Sit on the porch, lean back, and watch the clouds reshape themselves until something identifiable emerges.

* Meet a friend for a relaxed after-dinner conversation.

* Spend 15 minutes simply concentrating on the sounds you hear outside in your own backyard.

- Look at and smell every vegetable and piece of fruit you pick up before you put it in your shopping basket.

- Count the shades of green (or blue or red) you can see from your kitchen or office window.

- Bake a dessert just to enjoy the aroma, then deliver it to someone who won't expect it.

LaVerna Klippenstein
Published in *Christian Living* magazine

Gift of Simplicity

THE GIFT OF BEAUTY:

Remembering to enjoy
all of God's noble creation and all that
is good in man's artistic expression.

The Best Things in Life Are Nearest

Breath in your nostrils,

Light in your eyes,

Flowers at your feet,

Duties at your hand,

The path of right just before you.

ROBERT LOUIS STEVENSON
Novelist and world traveler

Discovering Joy

- Allow ourselves to complain of nothing, not even the weather.

- Never picture ourselves in any circumstances in which we are not.

- Never compare our lot with that of another.

- Never allow ourselves to wish that this or that had been otherwise.

- Never dwell on tomorrow; remember, that is God's and not ours.

E. B. PUSEY
English theologian

Silver Linings

Don't take yourself so seriously.

Thank God for the little things.

Look for an opportunity to help other people.

Choose joy.

Look for the silver lining in every gray cloud.

Add humor to conflicts and difficulties.

Don't base happiness on outward circumstances.

Don't try to be perfect.

Don't be easily offended.

Laugh every chance you get.

KEN DAVIS, COMEDIAN
Adapted from *Lighten Up!*

How to Be Really Content

Take the focus off yourself.

As long as you think about your personal contentment,
it will elude you.

Live free of debt.

Financial and emotional debt keep you trapped in the past.

Spend some time alone.

You need quiet time away from the hectic activities and noise
of life so you can find the peace of mind that comes with
internal silence.

Do something special for someone who is older.

Respect for and generosity toward those with more life
experience bring great satisfaction.

Keep young children in your life.

Children can teach you much about innocence, hope, joy, and simplicity.

Get involved in a worthwhile cause.

When you volunteer for something bigger than you, you realize that you really can make a difference.

Avoid negative people.

Negative people can steal contentment from the best of situations.

Discipline yourself.

Self-discipline gives you freedom. It helps you accomplish and enjoy those things that are truly important to you.

Understand the other person's point of view.

This will dissipate negative and energy-wasting emotional responses. It can also give you compassion, sensitivity, and sometimes even wisdom.

Treat yourself.

Occasionally it's nice to relax and remind yourself that you are a person of value and worth.

Be thankful for what you have.

The pursuit of pleasure is short-lived and never brings long-term satisfaction.

Ask for advice.

There is much you do not know, and seeking wisdom and/or direction from those around you can bring joys you never expected.

Avoid known temptations.

There are things in life that seem attractive but are actually dangerous and destructive. Flee them.

KAREN L. WILLOUGHBY
Editor and writing coach

How to Forfeit Peace

1. Resent God's ways.

2. Worry as much as possible.

3. Pray only about things you can't manage by yourself.

4. Refuse to accept what God gives.

5. Look for peace elsewhere than in Him.

6. Try to rule your own life.

7. Doubt God's Word.

8. Carry all your cares.

ELISABETH ELLIOT
From *Keep a Quiet Heart*

How to Find Peace

Great peace have they which love thy law:

and nothing shall offend them.

PSALM 119:165

King James Version

Don't worry over anything whatever.

PHILIPPIANS 4:6

Phillips Translation

In everything make your requests known to God

in prayer and petition with thanksgiving. Then the peace

of God...will keep guard over your hearts.

PHILIPPIANS 4:6–7

New English Bible

Take my yoke upon you and learn from me...

and you will find rest.

MATTHEW 11:29

New International Version

Peace is my parting gift to you,

my own peace, such as the world cannot give.

JOHN 14:27
New English Bible

Let the peace of Christ rule in your hearts.

COLOSSIANS 3:15
New International Version

Now the God of hope fill you

with all joy and peace in believing.

ROMANS 15:13
King James Version

Cast all your cares on him, for you are his charge.

1 PETER 5:7
New English Bible

VERSES SELECTED FROM THE BIBLE BY ELISABETH ELLIOT
From *Keep a Quiet Heart*

Gift of Simplicity

THE GIFT OF GENTLENESS:

*Treating others and
myself with patience, understanding,
and tenderness.*

Solitude Is a Place Where...

Meaning is found.

Truth is pondered.

Convictions are solidified.

Inspiration is born.

Visions are cast.

Character is developed.

Humility is learned.

Wrongs are forgiven.

Virtues are sought.

Demons are conquered.

Peace is embraced.

Love is nurtured.

Faith is enlarged.

Healing is discovered.

Joy is planted.

DR. STEVE STEPHENS
Psychologist and seminar speaker

The common tasks are beautiful
if we have eyes to see their shining ministry.
—GRACE NOLL CROWELL

In character, in manner, in style,
in all things, the supreme excellence is simplicity.
—HENRY WADSWORTH LONGFELLOW

Two wings lift a person up from earthly concerns:
simplicity and purity.
—THOMAS À KEMPIS

Silence

Sanctuary: Find a place free from distraction.

Invite new thoughts and the voice of God.

Listen and learn.

Evaluate emotions, ideas, dreams, convictions, and resolutions.

Never rush.

Confront challenging issues.

Ease back into your world with a plan of action.

CURTIS TUCKER
Pastor

ABC's of Thankfulness

Air and autumn and animals.

Babies and breath and beauty.

Children and compassion and creativity.

Daylight and dew and daffodils.

Emotions and energy and enthusiasm.

Faith and family and friends.

Grandparents and grandchildren and God.

Hands and health and hope.

Ice cream and intelligence and intuition.

Joy and journeys and jokes.

Kindness and kisses and kittens.

Love and laughter and leaves.

Mothers and music and memories.

Night and nature and neighbors.

Order and oranges and oceans.

Peace and patience and prayer.

Quiet and quality and questions.

Rain and rest and romance.

Sunshine and smiles and stars.

Time and teachers and trees.

Unity and understanding and uniqueness.

Vision and values and vacations.

Winter and water and wisdom.

e**X**citement and expression and experience.

Youth and yearning and yesterday.

Zest and zip and zeal.

TAMI STEPHENS
Mother of three

Joy for Today

I would like to read a noble poem.

I would like to see a beautiful picture.

I would like to hear a bit of inspiring music.

I would like to meet a great soul.

I would like to say a few sensible words.

GOETHE
Philosopher and playwright

Happiness

+ Happiness comes from spiritual wealth, not material wealth.

+ Happiness comes from giving, not getting.

+ If we try hard to bring happiness to others, we cannot stop
  it from coming to us also.

+ To get joy, we must give it.

+ To keep joy, we must scatter it.

JOHN TEMPLETON
From *More of the Best of Bits & Pieces*

Random Acts of Kindness

1. Let someone cut in front of you. 2. Send a thank-you note.

3. Take a bag of groceries to someone in need. 4. Volunteer.

5. Give a larger tip than normal. 6. Open a door for someone.

7. Visit the elderly. 8. Pick up litter. 9. Write a note of encourage-

ment to a teenager. 10. Invite a widow to dinner. 11. Be polite.

12. Take flowers to a neighbor. 13. Run errands for someone who

is sick. 14. Bake something for a friend. 15. Listen. 16. Watch

someone's children. 17. Ask, "What can I do for you?" 18. Invite

someone new for coffee. 19. Make a new employee feel welcome.

20. Smile at a stranger. 21. Be a Big Brother or Big Sister.

22. Help without being asked. 23. Compliment five people each

day. 24. Offer to pick up a neighbor's mail. 25. Talk respectfully.

26. Donate to a nonprofit organization. 27. Send a gift

anonymously. 28. Visit someone in the hospital. 29. Feed the

birds. 30. Do for others what you would like them to do for you.

ALICE GRAY, DR. STEVE STEPHENS, AND JOHN VAN DIEST

Caring for One Another

* Love one another.

* Be kind to one another.

* Honor one another.

* Encourage one another.

* Confront one another.

* Comfort one another.

* Serve one another.

* Be patient with one another.

* Forgive one another.

* Pray for one another.

SAINT PETER, SAINT PAUL, AND SAINT JAMES
Selected from *The Holy Bible*

Friendship Words

Concern

Courtesy

Contact

Caring

Comfort

Celebration

Cultivation

Connection

Continuity

Cherish

Companionship

Communication

Closeness

Consistency

EMILIE BARNES AND DONNA OTTO
From *Friends of the Heart*

Live Fully

* Feel your feelings—take responsibility for the content of your heart.

* Tell the truth—be vulnerable and truthful with others.

* Give it to God—ask for help from others and God, and recognize that you are needy and incapable on your own.

* Follow life's call—pursue your heart's desires.

* Submit to authority—recognize your limitations.

- Acknowledge that you matter—there is nothing you can do to be more or less loved by the One who made you.

- Recognize what you value—cherish it for what it is: a gift.

- Risk loss—you will find joy and success.

- Enjoy success—you will find more of God.

- Live fully.

CHIP DODD
Condensed from *The Voice of the Heart*

Love Is...

...asking about someone's day and truly caring about the answer.

...being patient, even when you're tired—especially when you're tired.

...writing a note of encouragement.

...buying someone flowers for no reason.

...caring—even when it's hard and you don't feel like it.

...trusting in someone even when you're scared.

...saying you're sorry when you are wrong.

...praying for someone.

...forgiving someone again and again.

...providing a shoulder to cry on.

...holding your tongue.

...what God does to us.

DANAE JACOBSON
Condensed from *Things I've Learned Lately*

Gift of Simplicity

THE GIFT OF HOPE:

*Looking forward to a future that
is better and brighter than anything
I have experienced today.*

We All Need…

To be loved…when lonely.

To be protected…when afraid.

To be comforted…when hurting.

To be fed…when hungry.

To be taught…when confused.

To be encouraged…when downhearted.

To be filled…when empty.

To be heard…when crying.

To be found…when lost.

To be given hope…when all seems dark.

DR. STEVE STEPHENS
Psychologist and seminar speaker

Understanding Hope

Hope works when riches fail.

Hope causes us to trust God's promises.

Hope looks beyond today's crushing problems.

Hope gives the farmer courage to plant, cultivate, and harvest.

Hope looks forward to spring in the midst of the harshest winter.

Hope believes that eternal life exists beyond the grave.

Hope keeps company with faith and love.

Hope is the reason we pray.

CHARLES B. DARLAND
Retired college professor

Understanding Faith

You will never learn faith in comfortable surroundings.

A. B. SIMPSON

Faith does not wait until it understands;

in that case it would not be faith.

VANCE HAVNER

Faith is saying "Amen" to God.

MERV ROSELL

A simple childlike faith…

solves all the problems that come to us.

HELEN KELLER

The only way to learn strong faith is to endure strong trials.

GEORGE MÜELLER

All work that is worth anything is done in faith.

ALBERT SCHWEITZER

Faith is not belief without proof, but trust without reservation.

D. ELTON TRUEBLOOD

Faith never knows where it is being led, but it loves and knows the one who is leading.

OSWALD CHAMBERS

Faith is knowing there is an ocean because you have seen a brook.

WILLIAM A. WARD

Faith is the conviction of realities I cannot see or feel.

PAMELA REEVE

A Prayer of Mother Teresa

Deliver me…

From the desire of being loved,

From the desire of being extolled,

From the desire of being honored,

From the desire of being praised,

From the desire of being preferred,

From the desire of being consulted,

From the desire of being approved,

From the desire of being popular,

From the fear of being humiliated,

From the fear of being despised,

From the fear of suffering rebukes,

From the fear of being calumniated,

From the fear of being forgotten,

From the fear of being wronged,

From the fear of being ridiculed,

From the fear of being suspected.

COMPILED BY LUCINDA VARDEY, EDITOR
From *Mother Teresa: A Simple Path*

Life Is Hard, but God Is Good

He is strong in our weakness.

He is comfort when we're in pain.

He is love when we need acceptance.

He is peace when we're haunted by fear.

He is protection when we're in trouble.

He heals our wounds when someone or something has hurt us.

He is our joy when our hearts are grieved.

He is our friend when we've been rejected.

He is our power when we need a miracle.

SHERI ROSE SHEPHERD
From *Fit for Excellence*

Gift of Simplicity

THE GIFT OF FAITH:

*Believing that God cares
for me deeply and wants me to rest
in the comfort of His love.*

Fear and Faith

Fear imprisons. *Faith* frees.

Fear troubles. *Faith* triumphs.

Fear cowers. *Faith* empowers.

Fear disheartens. *Faith* encourages.

Fear darkens. *Faith* brightens.

Fear cripples. *Faith* heals.

Fear puts hopelessness at the center of life. *Faith* puts fear
at the feet of God.

PHIL CALLAWAY
From *Who Put the Skunk in the Trunk?*

Be completely humble and gentle…

bearing with one another in love.

—PAUL THE APOSTLE

I am beginning to learn that

it is the sweet, simple things of life

which are the real ones after all.

—LAURA INGALLS WILDER

A sincere compliment is the

least expensive and most valuable gift

a person can offer.

—JOE TAKASH

Finding Humility in an Arrogant World

The humble can wait patiently,

while the arrogant want it now!

The humble demonstrate kindness,

while the arrogant don't even notice the need.

The humble are content, not jealous or envious,

while the arrogant feel they deserve more.

The humble honor and esteem one another,

while the arrogant brag on themselves.

The humble do not act unbecomingly,

while the manners of the arrogant are rude.

The humble show a servant spirit,

> *while the arrogant demand to be served.*

The humble are not easily provoked,

> *while the arrogant are quick to take offense.*

The humble quickly forgive a wrong suffered,

> *while the arrogant can't rest until they even the score.*

H. Dale Burke and Jac La Tour
From *A Love That Never Fails*

Eight Proven Steps toward Feeling Good

1. Learn to accept change.

2. Admit your weaknesses.

3. Ask for any help that you know you need.

4. Be open to solutions.

5. Deal directly with your problems.

6. Admit your faults.

7. Take full responsibility for your heart.

8. Tell the truth, especially to yourself.

CYNDI HAYNES
Condensed from *2,002 Ways to Cheer Yourself Up*

Gift of Simplicity

THE GIFT OF TRANQUILITY:

Watching the moon rise or
listening to the song of a meadowlark
until my soul is quieted.

A Positive Focus

Feel positive emotions.

Think positive thoughts.

Focus on the positive in people.

Offer positive prayers.

Speak positive words.

Practice positive actions.

RON JENSON
From *Taking the Lead*

Appreciating Good Days

- Give thanks, over and over again. Recognize the rarity and beauty of the gift. Appreciate it. Store the moments in your memory.

- Share the day with someone you love—either by doing something together or by telling somebody about it.

- Capture the good day for the future by writing in your journal, sketching the beauty around you, talking about it with your children.

- When the day is over, let it go with good grace. Smile and sigh and trust God for tomorrow.

EMILIE BARNES
From *A Cup of Hope*

Wisdom *for* Simple Living

How sweet it is
when the strong are also gentle.
—LIZZIE FUDIM

Where there is beauty apparent, we are to enjoy it;
Where there is beauty hidden, we are to unveil it;
Where there is beauty defaced, we are to restore it;
Where there is no beauty at all, we are to create it.
—ROBERT MCAFEE BROWN

Simplicity is the dream of
all who have too much to do.
—AUTHOR UNKNOWN

Slow Down And...

...walk in something soft with bare feet.

...touch a face with your eyes closed.

...watch the wind.

...feel your breath in your nostrils as you inhale and exhale.

...eat slowly and taste your food.

...feel your heart while you smile.

...smell flowers.

...listen to water.

...watch the moon rise.

...touch a baby.

LEE L. JAMPOLSKY
From *Smile for No Good Reason*

Stress Busters

⤏ Take a break.

⤏ Take a bath.

⤏ Take a walk.

⤏ Take a breath.

⤏ Take a nap.

JOHN VAN DIEST
Associate publisher

Eight Questions to Ask Before Saying Yes

1. Do I really understand this commitment?

2. How does this fit into my current goals and priorities?

3. Do I have the time, energy, and resources?

4. What impact will this have on me in a year? in five years? in ten years?

5. How will this impact those I love? Whom will it help? Whom will it hurt?

6. What do my friends and family think?

7. Can someone else do it better?

8. Do I really want to say yes?

ALICE GRAY
Seminar speaker

20 Ways to Simplify

1. Eliminate ten things from your life.

2. Cut back on TV.

3. Escape to a quiet spot.

4. Set your own pace.

5. Get rid of clutter.

6. When you bring in something new, throw out something old.

7. Do only one thing at a time.

8. Say no at least once a day.

9. Enjoy the little things.

10. Take at least four breaks per day.

11. Determine what really matters.

12. Make peace with all people.

13. Tell the truth.

14. Appreciate beauty.

15. If you don't need it, don't buy it.

16. If you don't have time, don't do it.

17. Have a place for everything, and put everything in its place.

18. Share your thoughts, feelings, and opinions with a friend every day.

19. Allow time to pray.

20. Thank God for what you have.

DR. STEVE STEPHENS
Psychologist and seminar speaker

Only Three Things You Need

→ A garden

→ A library

→ And someone to share them with.[1]

MARCUS TULLIUS CICERO
Statesman, philosopher, and orator

1. This line added by editors.

Gift of Simplicity

THE GIFT OF FORGIVENESS:

Understanding that as
I forgive others who have hurt me,
I release a burden that is too heavy
for me to carry.

20 Ways to Relax

1. Watch a sunrise at least once a year.

2. Learn to play a musical instrument.

3. Sing in the shower.

4. Never refuse homemade brownies.

5. Whistle.

6. Take someone bowling.

7. Sing in a choir.

8. Be romantic.

9. Buy a bird feeder and place it where it can be seen from your kitchen window.

10. Wave at children on school buses.

11. Lie on your back and look at the stars.

12. Rekindle old friendships.

13. Reread your favorite book.

14. Try everything offered by supermarket food demonstrators.

15. Never waste an opportunity to tell someone you love them.

16. Save one evening a week for just you and your spouse.

17. Begin each day with your favorite music.

18. Laugh a lot.

19. Give thanks for every meal.

20. Count your blessings.

H. JACKSON BROWN, JR.
Condensed from *Life's Little Instruction Book*

The contented man is never poor;

the discontented man, never rich.

—GEORGE ELIOT

Make the most of the best and the least of the worst.

—ROBERT LOUIS STEVENSON

Live simply; expect little;

give much; sing often; pray always.

—AUTHOR UNKNOWN

Entering into silence is like stepping into cool,

clear water. The dust and debris are quietly washed away,

and we are purified of our triviality.

—WENDY BECKETT

Seven Wonders of the World

1. Seeing

2. Hearing

3. Tasting

4. Touching

5. Running

6. Laughing

7. Loving

WRITTEN BY A LITTLE GIRL WHEN
HER TEACHER ASKED THE CLASS TO MAKE A LIST OF
THE SEVEN NATURAL WONDERS OF THE WORLD.

What to Think About

Let your mind dwell on these eight things...

Whatever is true

Whatever is noble

Whatever is right

Whatever is pure

Whatever is lovely

Whatever is admirable

Whatever is excellent

Whatever is praiseworthy

PHILIPPIANS 4:8
From *The Holy Bible*

Gift of Simplicity

THE GIFT OF SOLITUDE:

*Finding a time and place to
be alone so I can hear the still small
voice of God.*

15 Ways to Cheer Yourself Up

- Pat yourself on the back for all the many things you have done right in your life.

- Listen closely to the advice of loved ones.

- Ask everyone you know to tell you stories about miracles in their lives.

- Attend a benefit for a worthy cause.

- Reread your favorite childhood book before you drift off to sleep.

- Learn to laugh at yourself.

- Make definite plans for your immediate future.

- Say grace before each meal.

- Practice looking on the bright side of life.

- Make someone else feel valuable.

- Try to be happy about others' good fortune.

- Learn to accept compliments.

- Go somewhere you have never been.

- Do what you loved to do as a child.

- Let go of regrets.

CYNDI HAYNES
Condensed from *2,002 Ways to Cheer Yourself Up*

Wisdom *for* Simple Living

Take the gentle path.

—GEORGE HERBERT

'Tis a gift to be simple,
'Tis a gift to be free,
'Tis a gift to come down
Where we ought to be
And when we find ourselves
In the place that's right
'Twill be in the valley
Of love and delight.

—NINETEENTH-CENTURY HYMN

If I may only grow:
firmer, simpler, quieter, warmer.

—DAG HAMMARSKJÖLD

Be Good to You

Be yourself...truthfully.

Accept yourself...gratefully.

Value yourself...joyfully.

Forgive yourself...completely.

Treat yourself...generously.

Balance yourself...harmoniously.

Bless yourself...abundantly.

Trust yourself...confidently.

Love yourself...wholeheartedly.

Empower yourself...prayerfully.

Give of yourself...enthusiastically.

Express yourself...radiantly.

AUTHOR UNKNOWN

Keeping Joy

- Keep something green in a little vase or pot over your kitchen sink.

- Find a small gift book that lifts your spirits and gives you hope—one with prayers, affirmations, Scripture verses, or even just pretty pictures.

- Schedule a lunch break or an afternoon tea out with an encouraging friend.

- Spend an occasional lunch hour rocking newborns in a hospital nursery or volunteering at a day-care center.

- Find a lovely place where you can walk to boost your spirits—
  a park, an arboretum, a beautifully landscaped mall. Try to
  walk there at least once a week.

- Put together a collection of things that mean hope to you—
  pictures of your family, pebbles from a beach, a hank of kite
  string, a tulip bulb, or a miniature cross.

EMILIE BARNES
Condensed from *A Cup of Hope*

Day by Day

On this day…

I will try to be happy. My happiness is a direct result of my being at peace with myself; what others do or think will not determine my happiness.

On this day…

I will accept myself and live to the best of my ability.

On this day…

I will make time to pray and meditate on the Scriptures, seeking God and developing my relationship with Him.

On this day...

I will say what I mean and mean what I say.

On this day...

I will not tackle all my problems at once but live moment to

moment at my very best.

On this day...

I will live my life being assertive, not aggressive; being humble,

not proud; being confident to be exactly who I am.

On this day…

I will take care of my physical health. I will exercise my mind, my body, and my spirit.

On this day…

I will be kind to those around me. I will be agreeable, finding no fault with others. Nor will I try to improve or regulate others.

On this day…

I will remind myself that God has a special place in His heart for me and a special purpose for me to fulfill in this world.

CARL DREIZLER AND MARY E. EHEMANN
From *52 Ways to Lose Weight*

Essentials for Happiness

→ Something to do

→ Something to love

→ Something to hope for

JOSEPH ADDISON
Poet and essayist

Three Goals for My Life

1. To understand myself.

2. To see what God really wishes me to do.

3. To find the idea for which I can live and die.

SØREN KIERKEGAARD
Philosopher and theologian

Gift of Simplicity

THE GIFT OF PRAYER:

Remembering that
the most valuable gift for others
is often a dialogue between
my soul and God.

Things I Wish I'd Done Sooner

Not worried about the future when the present was real and alive before me.

Paid more attention when my parents and grandparents told about their past.

Hugged our children more.

Told my dad and other veterans how much I appreciate what they did for our country.

Taken more luxurious baths and read more captivating books.

Forgotten more grudges and given more forgiveness.

Used my antique teacups instead of just looking at them in the china hutch.

Gone to more operas, ballets, and concerts.

Worked less and played more.

Spent more time building friendships.

BARBARA M. DARLAND
Teacher, writer, artist

Gift of Simplicity

THE GIFT OF ENLIGHTENMENT:

*Allowing the light that lifts my
spirit to rekindle faith, hope, and love
in every aspect of my life.*

Habits to Nurture

Encourage one another.

Live in peace with each other.

Be patient with everyone.

Always try to be kind.

Be joyful evermore.

Pray continually.

In everything give thanks.

Hold on to good.

Avoid every kind of evil.

PAUL THE APOSTLE
Selected from *The Holy Bible*

Stay Young While Growing Old

1. Applaud the success of others.

2. Exercise daily.

3. Keep a positive attitude.

4. Read widely and often.

5. Play with children.

6. Enjoy nature.

7. Laugh heartily.

8. Take a class.

9. Plant a garden.

10. Count your blessings.

11. Take risks.

12. Sing from your heart.

13. Get a pet.

14. Eat healthily.

15. Give generously to others.

TRESS VAN DIEST
91 years young

Simple Ways to Be Romantic

Shower.

Wear perfume/cologne.

Dress nicely.

Floss and brush.

Keep a supply of breath mints, gum, and mouthwash handy.

Hold hands as much as possible.

Whisper "sweet nothings" in each other's ear.

Leave little love notes around the house,
in lunch bags, in cars, in purses.

Call for no reason.

Exercise.

Eat healthily.

Kiss a lot.

Share your deepest desires and dreams.

Be spontaneous.

Put the kids down early and eat supper late.

Invest in one of those "Romantic Love Songs" CDs.

Buy and burn some scented candles.

Stare into each other's eyes.

Stare into a fire together.

Share a blanket on the couch on a cold night.

Sit side by side on the couch.

Reminisce about your courtship.

Wink at each other.

Hug.

WOODS, HUDSON, DALL, AND LACKLAND
Condensed from *Marriage Clues for the Clueless*

Marriage Advice from 1886

Let your love be stronger than your hate or anger.

Learn the wisdom of compromise, for it is better to bend a little than to break.

Believe the best rather than the worst.

People have a way of living up or down to your opinion of them.

Remember that true friendship is the basis for any lasting relationship. The person you choose to marry is deserving of the courtesies and kindnesses you bestow on your friends.

Please hand this down to your children and your children's children: The more things change, the more they stay the same.

JANE WELLS
Wife and mother

Nothing Can Separate Us from God's Love

Not death

Not life

Not angels

Not demons

Not fears for today

Not worries for tomorrow

Not the greatest powers

Not the highest star

Not the deepest ocean

Not anything in all creation

PAUL THE APOSTLE
Adapted from Romans 8:38–39

Love...

Is very patient.

Is kind.

Is never jealous.

Is never envious.

Is never boastful.

Is never proud.

Is never haughty.

Is never selfish.

Is never rude.

Does not demand its own way.

Is not irritable or touchy.

Does not hold grudges.

Will hardly even notice when others do it wrong.

Is never glad about injustice.

Rejoices whenever truth wins out.

Is loyal no matter what the cost.

Will always believe.

Will always expect the best.

Will always defend.

Goes on forever.

PAUL THE APOSTLE
Adapted from 1 Corinthians 13:4–8

Try God

When troubles are deep and your world is dark,

Don't give up hope—TRY GOD.

When life turns sour and you've lost your way,

Don't give up hope—TRY GOD.

When fears stack up and you're sure no one cares,

Don't give up hope—TRY GOD.

When temptation comes knocking and you struggle so,

Don't give up hope—TRY GOD.

AUTHOR UNKNOWN

Wisdom for Simple Living

Appreciate simplicity.

—BRUCE AND STAN

*Simplicity is the difference
between just enough and too much.*

—AUTHOR UNKNOWN

*This should be your ambition:
to live a quiet life, minding your own business.*

—PAUL THE APOSTLE

A heart at peace gives life to the body.

—SOLOMON

12 Reasons to Pray

1. It encourages others.

2. It reminds you of spiritual values.

3. It gives hope.

4. It helps you feel better.

5. It allows you to let go of situations.

6. It provides comfort.

7. It relaxes you and reduces anxiety.

8. It builds faith.

9. It deepens character.

10. It broadens your perspective.

11. It brings you closer to God.

12. It works.

JOHN VAN DIEST
Board of Directors, Walk Thru the Bible Ministries

12 Things to Pray For

1. For a growing relationship with God

2. For positive relationships with your family members

3. For energy and enthusiasm for your work or career

4. For wisdom to make right and wise decisions

5. For your service to your church and community

6. For the special needs of your family and friends

7. For the spiritual lives of your church leaders

8. For wisdom for our government leaders

9. For the moral integrity of today's young people

10. For the safety of those serving in our armed forces

11. For a lasting peace among peoples and nations

12. For the opportunity to be a blessing to someone today

J. CARL LANEY
Professor of biblical literature, Western Seminary

The Mystery of Answered Prayer

I asked God for strength, that I might achieve;

I was made weak, that I might learn humbly to obey.

I asked for health, that I might do greater things;

I was given infirmity, that I might do better things.

I asked for riches, that I might be happy;

I was given poverty, that I might be wise.

I asked for power, that I might have the praise of men;

I was given weakness, that I might feel the need of God.

I asked for all things, that I might enjoy life;

I was given life, that I might enjoy all things.

I got nothing I asked for, but everything I had hoped for.

Almost despite myself, my unspoken prayers were answered.

I am, among men, most richly blessed.

At the end of the Civil War,
this prayer was found folded in the pocket of a Confederate soldier.

My List for Simplicity

Blessings I am thankful for...

_____

_____

_____

_____

_____

_____

_____

_____

_____

_____

My List for Simplicity

Regrets I need to release…

_____

_____

_____

_____

_____

_____

_____

_____

_____

_____

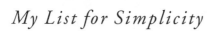

My List for Simplicity

Activities that bring me peace...

My List for Simplicity

Unimportant activities that I can remove from my schedule…

_____

_____

_____

_____

_____

_____

_____

_____

_____

_____

LISTS TO LIVE BY

My List for Simplicity

Books I'd like to read...

_____

_____

_____

_____

_____

_____

_____

_____

_____

_____

My List for Simplicity

Ways to bring me closer to God...

_____

_____

_____

_____

_____

_____

_____

_____

_____

My List for Simplicity

Dreams I'd like to pursue...

_____

_____

_____

_____

_____

_____

_____

_____

_____

_____

LISTS TO LIVE BY FOR EVERY MARRIED COUPLE

Offers tender, romantic, and wise ways to bring new life to marriage in a popular, easy-to-read format! This special collection of Lists to Live By is filled with gems of inspiration and timeless truths that married couples will treasure for a lifetime.
ISBN 1-57673-998-8

LISTS TO LIVE BY FOR EVERY CARING FAMILY

Provides inspiration on how to love, teach, understand, uplift, and communicate with children in topics such as "Helping Your Child Succeed," "Pray for Your Children," and "Four Ways to Encourage Your Kids." Parents will cherish each nugget of truth in this timeless special collection of Lists to Live By.
ISBN 1-57673-999-6

LISTS TO LIVE BY FOR SIMPLE LIVING

In our fast-paced, complex world, we all are looking for stillness, harmony, gentleness, and peace. The beauty of these eighty thoughtfully chosen lists is that they use simplicity to bring you simplicity—condensing essential information into one- or two-page lists.
ISBN 1-59052-058-0

LISTS TO LIVE BY FOR SMART LIVING

Reading a list is like having the best parts of a whole book gathered into a few words. Each list is a simple path to a better—smarter—life! If you read them, use them, and live them, you will become successful where it really matters—family, friendship, health, finance, business, wisdom, and faith.
ISBN 1-59052-057-2

Life-changing advice in a quick-to-read format!
LISTS TO LIVE BY

LISTS TO LIVE BY

This treasury of to-the-point inspiration—two hundred lists—is loaded with invaluable insights for wives, husbands, kids, teens, friends, and more. These wide-ranging ideas can change your life!
ISBN 1-57673-478-1

LISTS TO LIVE BY: THE SECOND COLLECTION

You'll get a lift in a hurry as you browse through this treasure trove of more *Lists to Live By*—with wisdom for home, health, love, life, faith, and successful living.
ISBN 1-57673-685-7

LISTS TO LIVE BY: THE THIRD COLLECTION

Two hundred lists with power, wisdom, inspiration, and practical advice. Some will make you reflect. Some will make you smile. Some will move you to action. And some will change your life.
ISBN 1-57673-882-5

THE STORIES FOR THE HEART SERIES

• More than 5 million sold in series!

• #1-selling Christian stories series!

Acknowledgments

Hundreds of books and magazines were researched, and dozens of professionals were interviewed for this collection. A diligent effort has been made to attribute original ownership of each list and, when necessary, obtain permission to reprint. If we have overlooked giving proper credit to anyone, please accept our apologies. If you will contact Multnomah Publishers, Inc., Post Office Box 1720, Sisters, Oregon 97759, with written documentation, corrections will be made prior to additional printings.

Notes and acknowledgments in this bibliography are shown in the order the lists appear and in the styles designed by the sources. For permission to reprint the material, please request permission from the original source. The editors gratefully acknowledge authors, publishers, and agents who granted permission for reprinting these lists.

Lists without attributions were compiled by the editors.